Oxford
Better
Spelling

OXFORD
UNIVERSITY PRESS

Great Clarendon Street, Oxford, OX2 6DP, United Kingdom

Oxford University Press is a department of the University of Oxford.
It furthers the University's objective of excellence in research, scholarship,
and education by publishing worldwide. Oxford is a registered trade mark of
Oxford University Press in the UK and in certain other countries

British Library Cataloguing in Publication Data

Data available

ISBN: 978-0-19-274322-0

1 3 5 7 9 10 8 6 4 2

Printed in Great Britain

Paper used in the production of this book is a natural,
recyclable product made from wood grown in sustainable forests.
The manufacturing process conforms to the environmental
regulations of the country of origin.

With thanks to Louise John for editorial support

Oxford OWL

For school
Discover eBooks, inspirational
resources, advice and support

For home
Helping your child's learning
with free eBooks, essential
tips and fun activities

www.oxfordowl.co.uk

Oxford Better Spelling

OXFORD

UNIVERSITY PRESS

Contents

Introduction

How to use this book

Better Spelling 2 has been written for children aged **9-11** to help them with their spelling. It is designed to be used to practise spellings they have already come across in their reading or learned in school.

The book is split into **3 sections**, for **9-year-olds**, **10-year-olds** and **11-year-olds**. For each age group, the words are arranged in groups of 5 for each day of the week from Monday to Friday. By following this simple '**5-a-day**' method, a child can learn 1000 words in 40 weeks!

Age	Number of weeks	Number of words
9	1-40	1000
10	1-40	1000
11	1-40	1000

At the end of each week, **5 words** are repeated at the bottom of the column to reinforce the spelling rules and patterns from that week.

At the end of each section, there are **3 sets** of engaging word activities to help with further practice. The **Now practise . . .** pages include themed groups of words from the words they have learned. The **Spelling help** pages reinforce common spelling rules. The **Word fun** pages contain word activities, such as solving anagrams and riddles and remembering how to spell words using word building and rhymes.

How are the words chosen?

The words in this book have been chosen according to the level appropriate for each age. The word groups become progressively more difficult as the child goes from **week 1** to **week 40**.

The aim of the book is to cover the variety of words and spelling patterns that a child of each age would expect to find in books, newspapers or websites suitable for that age. Additionally, it aims to build vocabulary and help children to decode more challenging words in their reading and writing. Essential words recommended for the relevant year group in the English national curriculum are also included.

This book includes many word forms and derivatives of words already learned in **Better Spelling 1**. Words that children frequently misspell have been identified using the **Oxford Children's Corpus.** Further information about the **Oxford Children's Corpus** is provided at the end of this book.

The best way to learn spelling is to learn little and often. This structured '**5-a-day**' approach provides children with practical support for learning to spell not only through the years of primary school but for lifelong reading and communication skills.

Spellings
for 9-year-olds

	Week 1	Week 2
Monday	sleeve knees banshee believed believing	dentist festival estimate downstairs upstairs
Tuesday	meeting reindeer reindeers creaked genuine	sandwich sandwiches snatching clenching twitching
Wednesday	cheerio programme programmed followed followers	pitcher creatures spinach teacher teaching
Thursday	tennis teddies stealth heather pleasant	scratched scratches chant enchanted fractured
Friday	spreading retell telling treasures treasured	switching adventures stretching stretched clutching

Spell it again . . .

believed • reindeer • programmed
pleasant • treasures

sandwiches • snatching
creatures • adventures
stretching

Week 3

Monday
gloves
fluffy
plumber
chuffed
lullaby

Tuesday
comrade
spotty
sponsor
watching
topping

Wednesday
surest
anomaly
shopping
swallowed
swallowing

Thursday
pottery
warren
honesty
biology
concrete

Friday
village
villager
villagers
worrier
fidgety

Week 4

Monday
tomatoes
groceries
approach
approached
volcanoes

Tuesday
hoping
billowing
bellowing
opponent
primrose

Wednesday
traitor
irritate
evaporated
slavery
enslave

Thursday
painter
painting
paintings
basement
apricot

Friday
creepy
tweeted
gleaming
nightie
families

plumber • sponsor
anomaly • swallowed
fidgety

groceries • volcanoes • apricot
creepy • families

	Week 5	**Week 6**
Monday	teapot teatime teaspoon almighty lifetime	overheard overhear lipstick aeroplanes grandad
Tuesday	sunbeam sunshine sunbathing treehouse greenhouse	minibus toadstool toadstools headline headlines
Wednesday	outside outstanding outback network workman	bitten pigeon ribbon chicken badminton
Thursday	rainbow raincoat raindrops rainforest password	zillion skeleton skeletons champion champions
Friday	birthday birthdays weekday everyday daylight	cauldron pelican companions scorpion scorpions

Spell it again . . .

almighty • treehouse • password
birthday • daylight

overheard • grandad
pigeon • companions
cauldron

Week 7

Monday
portion
edition
suction
audition
auditions

Tuesday
fraction
fractions
collection
collected
collecting

Wednesday
mentioned
fashioned
questions
questioned
magicians

Thursday
positions
positioned
occasion
direction
conditions

Friday
inventor
inventing
inventions
explosives
explosion

Week 8

Monday
strolling
sprint
responded
streaming
described

Tuesday
protested
suspected
encrusted
astounded
inspected

Wednesday
cascading
sprouting
respected
suspended
devastated

Thursday
scattered
scattering
standing
designer
designing

Friday
prisoner
remembers
wondering
defenders
defending

portion • questions
magicians • occasion
inventor

described • cascading • designing
devastated • sprouting

Week 9

Monday

pageant
pungent
jewellery
giraffe
journeyed

Tuesday

invade
breaker
payment
neighbours
behaviour

Wednesday

freezing
vividly
retrieve
adrenaline
enemies

Thursday

proceeded
succeeded
shrieking
screeched
screeches

Friday

activity
activities
penalties
abilities
factories

Week 10

entwine
fighting
diagram
society
paradise

analyse
wizened
tightened
apologise
apologised

realising
vibrating
cyclist
sightings
paralyse

surprises
exciting
gigantic
recognise
recognised

insect
neglect
conduct
compact
instinct

Spell it again . . .

pageant • neighbours • behaviour
shrieking • screeched

diagram • analyse
apologised • surprises
exciting

Week 11

Week 12

quieten
acquire
squash
squeaking
squealing

squeezing
squirting
squirming
squabbling
requested

garnet
mascara
sarcasm
sharpened
plastered

artist
parsley
parsnip
artefacts
avocado

bargain
parliament
harpoon
starting
argument

passenger
medicines
concerned
scientist
scientists

engross
fascinated
necklace
necklaces
classic

essence
romance
descended
princess
princesses

dressing
scissors
gossiping
assassins
especially

sceptre
centuries
announce
announced
announcing

quieten • squirting
artefacts • parliament
argument

scientist • fascinated • essence
descended • sceptre

	Week 13	Week 14
Monday	forlorn portrait sauntered performed performing	powdery drowning housing mountains mountainous
Tuesday	launching brought warlock explorer exploring	pounding shouldn't shoulder moustache encourage
Wednesday	applauded haunting monopolise monopolised nought	shouting favourites devouring yourself yourselves
Thursday	resources teleported astronaut support supported	thinking thicket therapy thousand thousands
Friday	sweeper cruiser confused possessed bemused	cruelty cruelly stiffen stiffly fiercely

Spell it again . . .

portrait • brought • applauded
resources • cruiser

mountainous • shouldn't
encourage • favourites
fiercely

Week 15

slightly	
slightest	
sneaker	
sneakily	
sneaked	

sincerely
accidentally
friendly
silently
normally

recently
sleepily
happily
bravely
exactly

obscure
injure
leisure
reassure
reassured

delicious
envious
marvellous
viscous
luminous

Week 16

youngest
countries
humongous
crunching
dungarees

remaining
equipped
forbidden
preparing
shrivelled

hammering
imagining
unwrapped
developed
committed

unravelled
traveller
travellers
travelling
travelled

mysteries
hypnotise
hypnotised
mystical
mythical

Monday

Tuesday

Wednesday

Thursday

Friday

sincerely • leisure
reassured • delicious
marvellous

countries • shrivelled • unwrapped
mysteries • hypnotised

	Week 17	**Week 18**
Monday	rattle rattling kettle particles colossal	squirrel squirrels struggle struggled struggling
Tuesday	bristle conical scuffle chortle shackle	scramble scrambled scrambling vegetable vegetables
Wednesday	triangle chemical chemicals tentacle tentacles	sensibly adorable capable lovable incredible
Thursday	obstacle obstacles valuable valuables hostile	excellent urgency incident entrance evidence
Friday	quarrel flannel colonel thimble utensil	absence distance hesitant hesitate hesitating

Spell it again . . .

colossal • bristle • valuables
quarrel • colonel

struggling • vegetables
excellent • absence
hesitant

Week 19

| Monday | Tuesday | Wednesday | Thursday | Friday |

Monday
tripping
spinning
knitting
stunning
trapper

Tuesday
dripping
splitting
wrapping
upsetting
throbbing

Wednesday
scrubbing
swimming
fitted
fitting
signalled

Thursday
planning
stripped
regretted
kidnapped
kidnappers

Friday
category
utility
allergy
rubbery
dignity

Week 20

Monday
fateful
referee
fitness
western
literacy

Tuesday
gleeful
privacy
miniscule
helpless
powerful

Wednesday
darkness
darkening
colourful
colouring
hurtful

Thursday
yoghurt
greyish
lemon
duchess
harmful

Friday
hateful
bubbly
tigress
trainee
training

knitting • swimming
signalled • category
allergy

referee • miniscule • literacy
colourful • darkening

	Week 21	Week 22
Monday	running peaceful anguish jumping hostess	confirmed surround surrounded returning murmuring
Tuesday	annoyed annoying destroyed destroying gargoyles	scurrying shuddered answering customers patterned
Wednesday	asteroid asteroids tortoise tortoises brightest	cucumber plunder survivor survivors surviving
Thursday	shooting footage mushrooms gruesome together	confronted confessed shuffling elephant elephants
Friday	continues continued continuing evacuate persuaded	defeating comforted handcuffs handcuffed snuffling

Spell it again . . .

anguish • gargoyles • asteroid
evacuate • continues

surround • answering
survivors • confessed
defeating

Week 23

Monday
armour
taller
butter
buttercup
buttercups

Tuesday
shutter
learnt
rumoured
raspberry
virtual

Wednesday
poverty
operate
dinosaur
stirrup
determined

Thursday
furnish
cleverest
surgeon
werewolf
werewolves

Friday
reporter
flavour
flavoured
firework
fireworks

Week 24

Monday
clambered
stammered
shattered
stuttered
whimpered

Tuesday
shimmered
slithered
slithering
scampered
scampering

Wednesday
smothered
flutter
fluttering
flickered
flickering

Thursday
glimmered
thundered
thundering
delivered
delivering

Friday
glittered
glittering
chattered
clattered
clattering

---

learnt • rumoured • surgeon
werewolves • flavoured

shimmered • flickering • smothered
delivering • chattered

	Week 25	**Week 26**
Monday	sheltered flustered splutter bewildered considered	language languages stranger strangers strangest
Tuesday	splatter splinter chuckling crackling cracking	building buildings spellings stockings happenings
Wednesday	pickles pickled sprinkle sprinkled trickling	exclaimed expecting explained explaining exploding
Thursday	attached cherish cheddar scrunched crouching	examining complex maximum umbrella crumpet
Friday	slouching chocolates challenge challenges exchange	stumbling crumbling crumpled plummeted plummeting

Spell it again . . .

bewildered • sprinkled • attached
crouching • exchange

languages • building
exclaimed • crumpled
plummeted

Week 27

Week 28

ancestors
listening
witnessed
menacing
sentenced

fencing
glistened
glistening
practised
replacing

crevice
advancing
ambulance
addressed
celebrated

artificial
crucial
decimal
criminal
initial

haven't
abandoned
attracted
activated
algebra

shivering
astonishing
finishing
demolish
splashing

thrashing
polishing
vanishing
shimmering
published

climbing
trembling
attempted
attempting
rampaging

pretended
pretending
belonging
reminding
pondering

revealing
retreated
repeating
retrieved
releasing

ancestors • glistened
artificial • abandoned
haven't

attempted • shimmering
rampaging • revealing
retrieved

	Week 29	Week 30
Monday	sometimes somebody bodyguards doughnuts chestnut	inhabit unwell including disabled discard
Tuesday	teenager hedgehog fairytale seatbelts eyelash	unloved distort impressed dispose disused
Wednesday	policemen gentlemen fishermen bathrooms classrooms	undress intruder disrupt understood mischief
Thursday	tiptoeing fingertips ladybirds rucksack cornflakes	disguise disguises unarmed introduce introduced
Friday	classmates spaceships waterfalls cartwheels motorbikes	unpacking disturbed imprisoned rebound distract

Spell it again . . .

sometimes • bodyguards • hedgehog
gentlemen • motorbikes

disabled • dispose • mischief
disguises • imprisoned

Week 31

Week 32

autographs
revolve
uncovered
discussed
discussing

piglet
tablet
suggest
suggested
exaggerate

restart
unleashed
dissolved
distress
paramedics

staggered
staggering
scraggy
swagger
magazine

recount
dismissed
unlocking
recovered
recovering

booklet
bracelet
ghost
sniggered
sniggering

resolve
disagreed
disobeyed
discovered
parachutes

baggage
rigging
ringlet
wriggling
triggered

proclaimed
lollipop
appearing
reappeared
disappears

guitar
fatigue
guardian
colleagues
intrigued

autographs • dissolved
disagreed • proclaimed
reappeared

exaggerate • magazine • baggage
fatigue • guardian

	Week 33	Week 34
Monday	overtake airline co-pilot percent jackpot	mystify mortify mummify terrified horrified
Tuesday	farewell warfare warship anything anywhere	magnifying petrified petrifying flattened blackened
Wednesday	inwards downwards afterwards catwalk catfish	barrack panicky panicked panicking knocking
Thursday	wardrobe payback boatman toyshop sandpit	attacking shrinking bickering nickname nicknamed
Friday	newborn newspapers newsagent midnight nightmares	climate situate educate decorate decorating

Spell it again . . .

anywhere • airline • wardrobe
newsagent • nightmares

terrified • magnifying
knocking • shrinking
situate

Week 35

Monday
cooker
stalker
snooker
daughter
daughters

Tuesday
twitter
laughter
reactor
flitter
register

Wednesday
predators
alligators
gangsters
computer
computers

Thursday
collapse
collapsed
collapsing
minutes
resident

Friday
movement
premise
detectives
relative
relatives

Week 36

Monday
evilest
strongest
prettiest
compost
complain

Tuesday
commanded
commented
commenced
completed
competing

Wednesday
dribbling
reflected
reflecting
strangle
strangling

Thursday
scribble
grappling
tingling
scrabbled
concluded

Friday
contacted
controlled
containing
contained
presented

stalker • daughter • laughter
collapsed • minutes

prettiest • commenced • grappling
controlled • containing

Week 37

Monday	snowball snowballs snowdrop snowflake snowflakes
Tuesday	footstep footsteps footballs footprints trapdoor
Wednesday	pineapple strawberry butterflies wetsuit rosebud
Thursday	walkway crowbar gumdrop demigod pigtail
Friday	keyring seasick seashore grandads whenever

Week 38

Monday	bluebell bluebells forecast suitcase suitcases
Tuesday	beehive fireball fireballs toolbox wandering
Wednesday	architect characters karaoke bracken bouquet
Thursday	liquorice monarch psychic conquered kangaroo
Friday	protected protecting predicted connected corrected

Spell it again . . .

trapdoor • pineapple • butterflies
seasick • whenever

suitcases • architect
bouquet • liquorice
conquered

Week 39

Monday
separated
glacier
premier
trampling
deflected

Tuesday
catapult
catapulted
eclipse
corridors
rummaging

Wednesday
communicate
carriage
drastic
steward
rasping

Thursday
dappled
muttering
stamina
angelic
restaurant

Friday
scuttling
daren't
crocodiles
humiliated
swivelled

Week 40

Monday
berserk
tadpole
vitamin
flounce
burrow

Tuesday
inferno
gryphon
squawking
anemone
alcohol

Wednesday
quivering
threaten
athletics
traipse
batteries

Thursday
granite
nemesis
daffodils
parasol
ornament

Friday
beckoning
squelching
deadliest
sapphire
mesmerised

premier • eclipse • carriage
restaurant • humiliated

berserk • gryphon • traipse
sapphire • mesmerised

Now practise . . .

Words to say instead of 'said'

apologised

questioned

described

screeched

requested

confessed

confirmed

reflected

chattered

stuttered

thundered

applauded

regretted

exclaimed

proclaimed

mentioned

protested

responded

reassured

announced

continued

delivered

predicted

stammered

whimpered

suggested

considered

explained

disagreed

sniggered

Now practise . . .

Strong adjectives

almighty

gigantic

wizened

squirming

peaceful

marvellous

humongous

mystical

adorable

lovable

excellent

gleeful

brightest

terrified

prettiest

pungent

exciting

squeaking

miniscule

luminous

delicious

forbidden

colossal

capable

incredible

bubbly

enchanted

cleverest

horrified

evilest

Spelling help

Tricky letters — ch, ph and sc

Sometimes the same letter groups can make different sounds. This can be confusing when you are learning and practising spellings.

- The letter group **ch** can make either a **/k/** sound, a **/sh/** sound or a **/ch/** sound.

- The letter group **sc** can make either an **/s/** sound or a **/sc/** sound.

- The letter group **ph** always makes an **/f/** sound.

Watch out for these letter groups in the words below:

gryphon	psychic	descended
elephants	cheerio	moustache
scratches	approach	architect
scattering	chortle	chemicals
obscure	autographs	monarch
fascinated	sapphire	enchanted
sceptre	cascading	chicken
parachutes	described	teacher
characters	scientists	

Spelling help

Tricky spellings

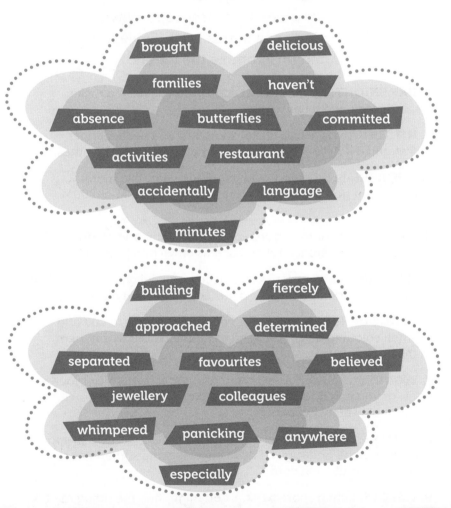

brought

delicious

families

haven't

absence

butterflies

committed

activities

restaurant

accidentally

language

minutes

building

fiercely

approached

determined

separated

favourites

believed

jewellery

colleagues

whimpered

panicking

anywhere

especially

Word fun

Sporty anagrams

These anagrams are made from sporty words you have learned to spell in this book. Solve the clues and unscramble the letters.

1. DAMBNIONT: For this racket sport, you will need a racket, a shuttlecock and a net to play.

2. NITSEN: This is also a racket sport, but you need a larger racket and a ball to play. Players normally wear white clothes.

3. GNINURN: In this sport, you might take part in a marathon or you might go for shorter distances, such as 100M or 200M on a track.

4. MMNGISIW: For this sport, you'll need water and plenty of it! You could try different strokes, such as crawl and butterfly.

5. NECFGIN: For this sport, you'll need a special type sword called a foil. You'll also need to wear a protective suit and mask.

6. NSOOEKR: To play this sport, you'll need a table, a cue and lots of small coloured balls. You need to hit the balls and get them in the pockets!

7. BLGINCIM: You can do this sport outdoors on cliffs or mountains, or you can do it indoors on specially made walls. You'll need ropes and a safety helmet.

8. EERFERE: I am the person who is in charge of fairness in sports, such as football and rugby. I have a whistle and sometimes a yellow card and a red card.

9. YCILCTS: I am a sportsperson. You might find me riding my bike on the road or in a velodrome.

*Answers at the bottom of p.35

Word fun!

Building words

Sometimes words can be combined together to build new words! Here are some compound words you have already learned in this book. See if you can think of any more words like these. Look at the words you have joined together to help you spell the new word.

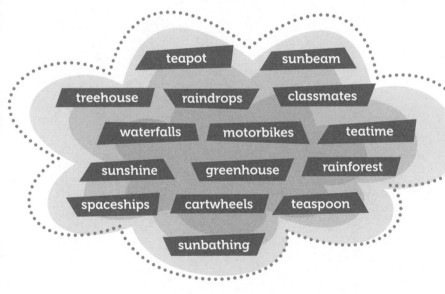

teapot

sunbeam

treehouse

raindrops

classmates

waterfalls

motorbikes

teatime

sunshine

greenhouse

rainforest

spaceships

cartwheels

teaspoon

sunbathing

Answers to anagrams on p.34:
1. badminton 2. tennis 3. running 4. swimming 5. fencing 6. snooker 7. climbing 8. referee 9. cyclist

Spellings
for 10-year-olds

	Week 1	Week 2
Monday	banner dazzling mammal jagged valley	slammed slamming snapped snapping snatched
Tuesday	arid stabbed annual wagon saps	plaits wax fabulous tank splashed
Wednesday	tan tattered avenue smack mattress	acid examined gap splattered patterns
Thursday	clamp banister madam traffic pansy	latch enact battling grabbing relaxing
Friday	cap flapping strapped clapping happiest	bud suffered insult fluttered customer

Spell it again . . .

mammal • annual • avenue
traffic • happiest

snatched • plaits • fabulous
suffered • customer

Week 3

Monday
hum
hunch
plump
repulsive
dusk

Tuesday
spun
chucked
thump
slump
utter

Wednesday
suddenly
clung
flung
spluttered
skull

Thursday
lug
summit
muscle
muscular
mushroom

Friday
adjusted
bungalow
hurriedly
interrupt
struck

Week 4

Monday
kid
ached
chorused
rake
hockey

Tuesday
ash
shivered
astonished
shrill
shove

Wednesday
flesh
brushing
demolished
shopper
polished

Thursday
duo
damage
challenged
marriage
generous

Friday
image
digit
prejudice
privilege
dodge

repulsive • chucked • muscle
bungalow • hurriedly

ached • chorused • marriage
generous • privilege

	Week 5	Week 6
Monday	passengers messenger carriages carried jazz	fee exceed beaker deceive envy
Tuesday	porridge rigid savage strangely legible	speaker era repeated breed priest
Wednesday	sausages villages dungeons giraffes jubilant	keen pierce fleece revealed belief
Thursday	surrender September October November December	beady east thirteen eighteen query
Friday	bubbling dangling tumbling giggling rumbling	needle speeding greet bunnies magazines

Spell it again . . .

porridge • sausages • dungeons
December • tumbling

exceed • deceive • priest
eighteen • bunnies

Week 7

Monday
sneaking
career
nosey
nosy
Greek

Tuesday
crease
bodies
peered
screeching
fields

Wednesday
unclear
clearing
steaming
relieved
dreary

Thursday
berries
weaken
weakness
cleaning
features

Friday
treating
treatment
released
buried
deceased

Week 8

Monday
daisies
machines
ladies
memories
mummies

Tuesday
width
widen
irate
shining
riot

Wednesday
dire
sympathise
grime
enquired
lined

Thursday
supply
supplies
replies
applied
spied

Friday
strident
improvise
bride
china
deciding

crease • fields • relieved
berries • buried

daisies • sympathise • supplies
spied • improvise

	Week 9	Week 10
Monday	wove flowing tone poachers stroking	wry admiring sighed fiery variety
Tuesday	toasted envelope soda opponents noticing	paralysed ivy lively identity pride
Wednesday	expose loaf indigo yoga global	trying spiteful slimy lighting ion
Thursday	willow clothing dome progress rodent	occupy pine brightly brighter file
Friday	sofa poked yoke sole choked	lime survival whine fire isolated

Spell it again . . .

envelope • opponents • global
progress • choked

wry • fiery • paralysed
survival • isolated

Week 11

Monday

glide
disguised
entire
entirely
ignite

missiles
spine
reunited
agile
sacrifice

bathe
grain
essay
trailing
elevator

laces
estate
occasionally
rotate
blade

state
statement
evacuated
haze
hazel

Week 12

bracelets
vain
chasing
navy
trace

evade
engraved
tape
curator
range

hatred
cradle
arranged
rate
pavement

mace
fate
phrase
apex
translate

complained
fountain
remained
trainers
mainly

disguised • sacrifice • elevator
occasionally • evacuated

evade • curator • phrase
translate • remained

	Week 13	Week 14
Monday	chin research clenched chopped checking	touching signature crouched ventured catchment
Tuesday	pinch exchanged fixture cherry drenched	fool foolish issue balloons goodness
Wednesday	chanting chuckled chatting matching munching	maroon swooping fluid intruders instrument
Thursday	birch pitched chickens departure trenches	smooth smoothie bruise superior looking
Friday	searching stitched marching punching chopping	soothe included assure assurance reassurance

Spell it again . . .

exchanged • research • departure
stitched • chopping

signature • crouched • fluid
bruise • reassurance

Week 15

tune
stupidly
acute
assume
produced

security
volume
individual
community
common

opportunity
individuality
arguments
arguable
unarguable

costumes
circling
circular
students
studying

area
index
beware
debt
rarely

Week 16

epic
sweater
depth
pelt
dairy

onset
lemonade
wealthy
steadily
dreamt

definite
cellar
effect
carefully
heaven

lisp
cygnet
infant
system
bandit

slid
swift
vicar
rhythm
spirits

Monday
Tuesday
Wednesday
Thursday
Friday

assume • community
circular • studying
debt

sweater • dreamt • definite
cygnet • rhythm

	Week 17	Week 18
Monday	pyramids olive worrying print crisp	Monday Tuesday Wednesday Thursday Friday
Tuesday	dart salmon varnish guarantee remarked	incredibly discovery distressed distracted subtract
Wednesday	cargo almond guardians sparkled target	Saturday Sunday January May August
Thursday	starry embarrass embarrassment apartment standard	squashing squashed equip equipped squinted
Friday	brass canal cinema clasp album	equator quadrant quotable consequent infrequent

Spell it again . . .

olive • salmon • embarrassment
guardians • cinema

Wednesday • January
equipped • quotable
infrequent

Week 19

unpopular
underwear
undergrowth
conifer
paragraph

unpacked
transform
transparent
underwent
development

recommend
represent
residents
unnatural
replaced

hospital
hostel
pimple
cancel
invisible

physical
sprinkles
tropical
strangles
freckles

Week 20

sandals
nostrils
crystals
controls
thistle

idle
idol
metal
ruffle
rifle

spectacle
scribbled
horrible
horribly
horrific

senses
sensible
terrible
terribly
symbol

pert
curtain
purchase
urgent
occur

undergrowth • transparent
recommend • tropical
strangles

crystals • thistle • horribly
symbol • occur

	Week 21	Week 22
Monday	alert permanent bothered eternity scurried	deserted inserted intern Italian perceive
Tuesday	blurred figures acre rounders centimetres	German personal bursting servants hurtling
Wednesday	current currant murdered urban turquoise	surprising deserved wandered wondered wonderful
Thursday	upper sturdy injury injuries church	owlet account accountant trousers amount
Friday	swirling battered wintry controversy properly	pounce county doubt floury frowned

Spell it again . . .

scurried • centimetres • turquoise
injuries • controversy

Italian • perceive • surprising
accountant • frowned

Week 23

grounded
bouncing
counting
crowding
lounge

bitter
crater
factor
otter
splintered

sinister
minister
ancestor
shoulders
bewilders

prisoners
minor
visitors
visited
visiting

foreign
dolphins
fanciful
infested
feathers

Week 24

sapphires
flicking
engulfed
sniffing
confront

blocking
stepping
dreading
escaping
twisting

grinning
glinting
arriving
clinging
watering

pressing
swinging
scanning
avoiding
spitting

stinging
gripping
hovering
dragged
dragging

Monday
Tuesday
Wednesday
Thursday
Friday

crowding • ancestor • shoulders
feathers • foreign

sapphires • confront • dreading
avoiding • dragged

	Week 25	**Week 26**
Monday	borough plough bough thorough coughing	mourn corridor forwards coarse orbit
Tuesday	sought fawn glorious supporting storey	swarmed tortured launched smallest according
Wednesday	warriors courteous dawn floral hoarse	divorced forcible enforce quartet quarters
Thursday	scorch crawling clause inform informed	explorers explored reporters reported ignoring
Friday	fourteen malt ornaments boarding portraits	cotton rotten frighten threat threatened

Spell it again . . .

thorough • glorious • hoarse
fourteen • portraits

corridor • according
reporters • cotton
frighten

Week 27

Monday
conceive
aggressive
response
necessary
secondary

Tuesday
assembly
cities
citizens
stressed
convince

Wednesday
cemetery
slippers
slippery
slipping
accepted

Thursday
ascend
novice
harass
glancing
insisted

Friday
casual
dismal
crime
criminals
original

Week 28

Monday
stallion
delicate
galloped
relevant
military

Tuesday
mouldy
brilliant
electrical
twelfth
desolate

Wednesday
smelling
lollipops
delivery
talent
thrilled

Thursday
elves
noises
assesses
positive
blizzard

Friday
penguins
siblings
whispers
whizzing
poisoned

aggressive • assembly
ascend • casual
original

galloped • mouldy • assesses
blizzard • whispers

Week 29

Monday

overcome
armchair
notebook
fearsome
lifeboat

Tuesday

driveway
motorway
wildlife
chainsaw
campsite

Wednesday

pancakes
internet
bedrooms
unicorns
goodbyes

Thursday

mermaids
cupcakes
coconuts
weekends
passport

Friday

weirdest
greatest
scariest
medium
period

Week 30

knocked
knot
rustling
solemn
whistled

impact
desperate
constant
admit
admitted

instant
instincts
sprinting
pregnant
parent

transfer
transferring
transferred
hesitated
hesitancy

refer
referral
referred
referring
reference

Spell it again . . .

fearsome • wildlife • goodbyes
weirdest • scariest

solemn • desperate
transfer • referral
whistled

Week 31

hind
hindrance
assist
assistant
assistance

performance
preferring
preference
innocent
innocence

decent
decency
frequent
frequency
frequently

competent
competence
coincidence
independence
existence

cheerful
grateful
hopeless
meanness
thoughtful

Week 32

lifeless
joyfully
restless
practically
gosling

spotless
secretly
fondly
duckling
bringing

visibly
possibly
environment
punishable
punishment

staring
gingerly
blinding
disaster
disastrous

honestly
movements
shocking
furiously
drifting

Monday

Tuesday

Wednesday

Thursday

Friday

assistance • preferring
frequently • thoughtful
independence

practically • possibly • environment
disastrous • furiously

	Week 33	Week 34
Monday	breakfast highlight inland interview mastermind	arrested stunned prepared trembled trickled
Tuesday	milkshake nonsense offspring ourselves overjoyed	snuggled shuffled stranded grumbled involved
Wednesday	photocopy photograph pinstripe earthquake throughout	shrugged scuttled compared invented wrinkled
Thursday	unison doorbell rucksacks platform backpack	crumbled wriggled pondered glimpsed summoned
Friday	hedgehogs wherever overhead doorstep handcuff	contents blankets biscuits expand expensive

Spell it again . . .

interview • earthquake • throughout
hedgehogs • wherever

wrinkled • wriggled
glimpsed • biscuits
expensive

Week 35

Monday
adorably
changeable
noticeable
dependable
reasonable

Tuesday
available
vulnerable
memorable
understand
understandable

Wednesday
co-ordinate
co-operate
co-own
correspond
committee

Thursday
repair
returned
re-enter
entered
entering

Friday
ambitious
fictitious
nauseous
nutritious
voluminous

Week 36

Monday
conscience
conscious
cautious
caution
malicious

Tuesday
infected
infectious
social
partial
essential

Wednesday
official
officers
confident
confidential
confidence

Thursday
utterance
substance
specially
appreciate
locate

Friday
solution
reactions
politicians
impression
dictionary

changeable • available
co-ordinate • nauseous
nutritious

conscience • cautious • specially
appreciate • dictionary

	Week 37	**Week 38**
Monday	instruct instructor instruction national operation	decoration decorated explanation conversation celebration
Tuesday	creating creative creation emotions directions	protection observed observant observance observatory
Wednesday	description profession commotion attraction missions	expectant expectation tolerant tolerance toleration
Thursday	option addition multiplication reduce reduction	applicable applicably application tolerable tolerably
Friday	faction receipt reception reject rejection	considerable considerably consideration attend attention

Spell it again . . .

instructor • profession • commotion
multiplication • receipt

conversation • observant
applicable • considerably
attention

Week 39

Week 40

Monday · Tuesday · Wednesday · Thursday · Friday

Monday
- grapefruit
- toenail
- fingernail
- fortnight
- download

- telescope
- negative
- analogue
- boulders
- beckoned

Tuesday
- eardrum
- outlaw
- blackbird
- headache
- sunflower

- accompany
- intrigue
- ecstatic
- secretary
- handsome

Wednesday
- basketball
- baseball
- overall
- greyhound
- eyesight

- helicopter
- government
- ceremony
- librarian
- certificate

Thursday
- wallpaper
- teacup
- eyelashes
- eyelid
- eyebrows

- accommodate
- kangaroos
- rhubarb
- dominoes
- wisdom

Friday
- daydream
- moonlight
- sunlight
- teenagers
- forehead

- amateur
- technique
- enjoyable
- vulnerable
- pronunciation

fortnight • headache eyesight • wallpaper forehead

boulders • intrigue • government rhubarb • accommodate

Now practise . . .

Watch out for double letters!

dazzling

jagged

annual

strapped

challenge

meanness

assistance

suffered

interrupt

marriage

messenger

giraffes

community

accountant

brilliant

mammal

valley

tattered

happiest

referring

practically

grabbing

summit

shrill

occupy

porridge

opponent

reassurance

necessary

assesses

Now practise . . .

Making adverbs with -ly

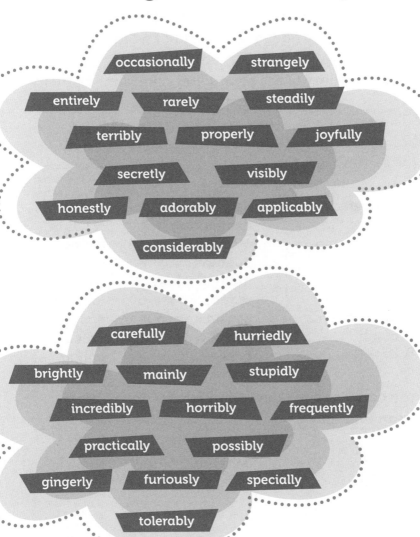

occasionally   strangely

entirely   rarely   steadily

terribly   properly   joyfully

secretly   visibly

honestly   adorably   applicably

considerably

carefully   hurriedly

brightly   mainly   stupidly

incredibly   horribly   frequently

practically   possibly

gingerly   furiously   specially

tolerably

Spelling help

Spelling the sound /shun/

The sound **/shun/** can be spelled in different ways.
It is normally added to the end of words as a suffix.
You have already learned lots of words that use
this spelling of the sound. Here are some of them
for you to practise again.

Words that end in **-t** or **-te** use the spelling **-tion**
for the sound **/shun/**:

decoration	description	reaction
instruction	commotion	solution
explanation	attraction	caution
caution	addition	rejection
operation	multiplication	faction
celebration	reduction	toleration
protection	consideration	application
creation	attention	expectation
direction	conversation	option

You can also spell the sound **/shun/** using **-ssion**,
-sion and **-cian**.

profession	occasion	magician
mission	explosion	politician

Spelling help

Tricky spellings

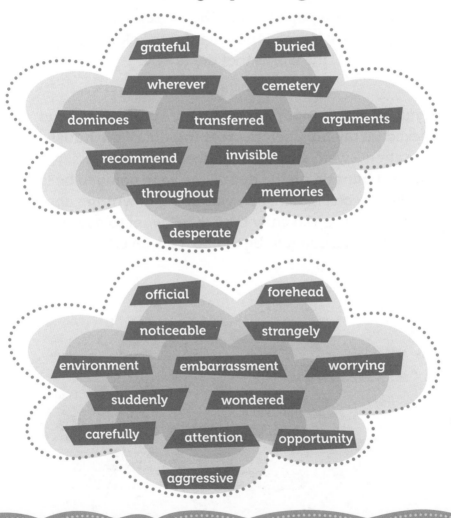

grateful

buried

wherever

cemetery

dominoes

transferred

arguments

recommend

invisible

throughout

memories

desperate

official

forehead

noticeable

strangely

environment

embarrassment

worrying

suddenly

wondered

carefully

attention

opportunity

aggressive

Based on the Oxford Children's Corpus research and analysis. See pp94-95 for more information.

Word fun

Fun with synonyms!

Read the paragraph below. Choose some of the new words you have learned to spell from the cloud to replace the words that are in bold.

I grabbed my **jumper,** pulled on my **sports shoes** and picked up my **bag**, before **creeping** out of the **house**. The streets were **empty** as I jogged towards Ben's house. I **banged** on the door – we were going to be late for the football match. Ben was going to **whinge** about having to get up so early but I didn't want to have a **row**. This was going to be the **best** day ever!

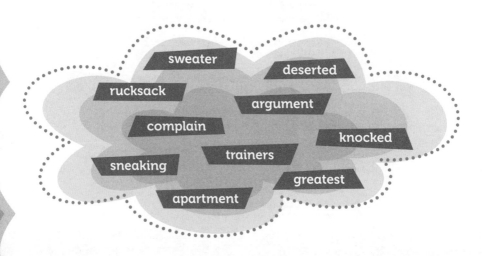

sweater

deserted

rucksack

argument

complain

knocked

trainers

sneaking

greatest

apartment

Word fun

All words with 'all'

Look again at the words you have learned to spell
and see if you can spot all the 'alls' in them!
Remember, you might find them in the middle
of the words, not just at the end.

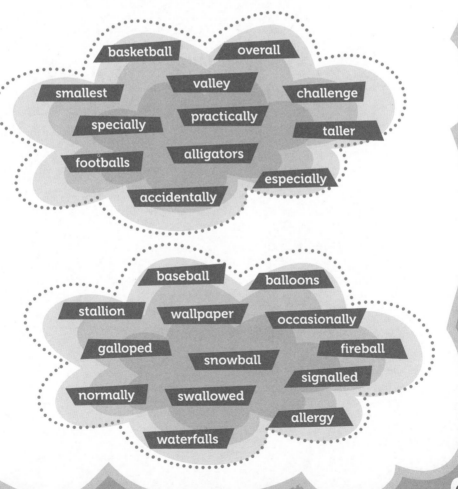

basketball   overall

smallest   valley   challenge

specially   practically   taller

footballs   alligators   especially

accidentally

baseball   balloons

stallion   wallpaper   occasionally

galloped   fireball

snowball   signalled

normally   swallowed

allergy

waterfalls

Spellings
for 11-year-olds

	Week 1	Week 2
Monday	treaty treatable untreatable squealed deceitful	sage cartilage postage drudge religious
Tuesday	squeaked steeple appearance disappearing disappearance	management manageable unmanageable refuge judgement
Wednesday	easel seedling abbey defeated undefeatable	digestion digestible indigestible rummaged region
Thursday	wreath shrieked received weal stampede	imaginable imagination unimaginable lodging jockey
Friday	bleached siege steepest persevere perseverance	encouraged encouragement logical orphanage agitated

Spell it again . . .

deceitful • disappearance
wreath • shrieked
perseverance

religious • unmanageable
indigestible • region
encouragement

Week 3

beverage
singe
salvage
salvageable
unsalvageable

strategy
trudged
partridge
majority
genre

cartridge
magically
legendary
privileged
gorgeous

sergeant
dodged
longitude
majestic
eligible

edgy
forge
joint
grudge
magi

Week 4

delighted
enlightenment
frightening
thyme
terrifying

client
purify
wives
spies
refined

inscribe
solidify
civilised
clarify
dimension

divert
divergent
pliant
pliable
compliant

liable
reliable
unreliable
reliant
stile

salvageable • trudged
privileged • sergeant
magi

thyme • client
dimension • compliant
unreliable

	Week 5	Week 6
Monday	ranch clutched switched merchant chapel	multiply grimy pylon lithe primate
Tuesday	yearn verse burying suburb excursion	victorious mischievous previous miscellaneous industrious
Wednesday	hurricane perfection murmured glittery alliteration	odorous ridiculous numerous numeracy innumerable
Thursday	interminable indeterminable determination occurred occurrence	heir healthier despairing pheasant tremor
Friday	internal scarpered worriedly rehearsed preserve	delve threatening remedy irremediable tepid

Spell it again . . .

switched • burying
murmured • occurrence
worriedly

pylon • mischievous
miscellaneous • healthier
irremediable

Week 7

presence
presentable
airy
feral
deafening

unnecessary
necessity
millionaire
error
elevate

kayak
trek
orchestra
melancholy
piquant

scholar
attacked
chasm
conqueror
unconquerable

kidney
realistic
cogent
graphic
skipped

Week 8

maim
portray
taper
tailor
articulate

wavy
situated
claimed
reclaim
irreclaimable

slain
remainder
maintain
maintenance
ornate

complaint
patriot
gladiator
brainy
staying

obtain
obtainable
domain
abbreviate
detailed

Monday
Tuesday
Wednesday
Thursday
Friday

unnecessary • millionaire
orchestra • unconquerable
cogent

articulate • maintenance
complaint • patriot
abbreviate

	Week 9	**Week 10**
Monday	oboe furrow loath nomad nomadic	covenant unofficial opulent topical opportune
Tuesday	moat lowly supposed overt notable	abolish offended florist optical optician
Wednesday	towing strode goad deodorant donor	opposition observation unobservant mottled optimistic
Thursday	approaching approachable irreproachable unapproachable modem	obtuse occupation occupant oracle orator
Friday	spat salary pallid advertise advertisement	hovel novel prospect clarinet trumpet

Spell it again . . .

furrow • supposed
deodorant • irreproachable
advertisement

unofficial • opportune
unobservant • occupation
clarinet

Week 11

Monday
employer
employment
unemployment
unemployable
embroidered

Tuesday
appoint
appointment
loiter
poised
flamboyant

Wednesday
ointment
deployment
enjoyment
unavoidable
clairvoyant

Thursday
taut
swore
format
applause
authority

Friday
organisation
tournament
cautiously
formidable
astronauts

Week 12

Monday
automatically
appalled
naught
warrant
distraught

Tuesday
audio
audience
audible
inaudible
falter

Wednesday
exhausted
inexhaustible
exorbitant
absorbent
informant

Thursday
mince
suspense
ounce
rancid
condense

Friday
remembrance
sensory
stance
instance
circumstance

embroidered • appointment
clairvoyant • applause
cautiously

automatically • distraught
inexhaustible • absorbent
circumstance

Monday

Week 13	Week 14
quaver	temperature
quarry	miniature
equipment	virtue
acquainted	altitude
acquaintance	salute

Tuesday

Week 13	Week 14
quilted	humour
equivalent	tributary
delinquent	fortunately
questionable	unfortunately
unquestionable	vacuum

Wednesday

Week 13	Week 14
effervescent	curiosity
aggressively	curiously
procession	latitude
pessimistic	individuality
centenary	pendulum

Thursday

Week 13	Week 14
electricity	persuade
passable	argumentative
trespassing	gradual
impassable	moist
unsurpassable	moisture

Friday

Week 13	Week 14
fluorescent	factual
oppressed	accurate
irrepressible	mutiny
placid	continually
piercing	lieutenant

Spell it again . . .

acquaintance • delinquent
effervescent • unsurpassable
fluorescent

temperature • humour
unfortunately • continually
lieutenant

Week 15

resistant
resistance
regent
regency
insurance

defiant
defiance
consultant
consultancy
annoyance

clemency
inclement
intolerant
intolerance
pregnancy

defendant
self-defence
reverent
reverence
acquaintance

decadent
decadence
vehement
vehemence
coincidence

Week 16

adept
abrupt
acceptance
acceptable
unacceptable

sprig
simile
whipped
metallic
continent

amphibian
whimpering
emigrate
immigrant
emigrant

vigorously
intimate
literally
platinum
flimsy

dinghy
navigate
lavish
hinder
witty

Monday

Tuesday

Wednesday

Thursday

Friday

insurance • consultant
self-defence • acquaintance
coincidence

unacceptable • whipped
vigorously • dinghy
literally

	Week 17	Week 18
Monday	flume suited suitable unsuitable wouldn't	insolent insolence vacant vacancy truancy
Tuesday	troupe congruent rumours putting enthusiastically	diligent diligence eminent eminence ambience
Wednesday	ambush festooned bruises recruitment exclude	differ difference indifferent indifference pestilence
Thursday	fulfilling fulfilment moving translucent denouement	unimportant importance incompetent incompetence prevalence
Friday	pastry pastries assailant entertainment containment	fragrant fragrance impertinent impertinence providence

Spell it again . . .

unsuitable • congruent
enthusiastically • recruitment
denouement

ambience • indifferent
unimportant • prevalence
impertinent

Week 19

distinguish
distinguishable
indistinguishable
guarding
guidance

extinguish
inextinguishable
gullible
unguessable
pentagon

funnel
clamour
glutton
nourish
frustrated

shoved
flushing
accustomed
illustrate
frumpy

conductor
senior
familiar
governor
ungovernable

Week 20

lavender
infer
hamper
professor
professional

sprang
lengthen
mending
mapping
whispering

defect
fragment
fragmented
atmosphere
refreshment

alphabet
sufficient
insufficient
satisfactory
welfare

laughing
laughable
triumphant
figment
affable

indistinguishable • gullible
clamour • accustomed
conductor

laughing • professional
whispering • insufficient
triumphant

	Week 21	Week 22
Monday	indulge indulgent indulging indulgence self-indulgence	spherical cathedral flexible inflexible gaggle
Tuesday	dormant dormancy reluctant reluctance excellence	insensible respectable vertical miserable fictional
Wednesday	arrogant arrogance prudent imprudent prudence	discomfort comfortable uncomfortable creditable discreditable
Thursday	attendant attendance sequence subsequent consequence	halved garment medallion embarrassed parchment
Friday	emergent emerged emergence emergency vibrancy	apparent department compartment gallant talents

Spell it again . . .

self-indulgence • excellence
attendant • subsequent
emergency

inflexible • miserable
discreditable • embarrassed
gallant

Week 23

pardon
pardonable
unpardonable
sarcastically
participant

method
welcomed
muttered
compound
mumbled

wrapped
honoured
honourable
settled
settlement

specialised
diminish
establish
establishment
machinery

accomplish
accomplishment
banishment
shipment
missionary

Week 24

investigate
immediately
disinfectant
nonchalant
miscreant

mistrust
untrustworthy
pronounce
pronouncement
abseil

abstract
attractive
recollect
collectable
collectible

coherent
incoherent
explicit
explicable
inexplicable

assignment
bewilderment
uncontrollable
explosions
absent

sarcastically • honourable
specialised • accomplishment
missionary

disinfectant • untrustworthy
attractive • inexplicable
uncontrollable

77

	Week 25	**Week 26**
Monday	fluent affluent fluency influence radiance	donation dalmatian pension succession martians
Tuesday	fragrant fragrance existent non-existent non-existence	expedition appreciation destruction destructible indestructible
Wednesday	efficient efficiency elegant inelegant elegance	introduction production affection separation congregation
Thursday	ignorant ignorance dominant dominance residence	association exhibition applicant apprentice appliance
Friday	potent potency vigil vigilant vigilance	imitation inimitable exception exceptionable unexceptionable

Spell it again . . .

affluent • non-existent
efficiency • ignorant
vigilance

appreciation • indestructible
separation • applicant
unexceptionable

Week 27

Monday
sympathy
boundary
variation
variable
variance

Tuesday
responsible
responsibility
accompanying
eventually
contentedly

Wednesday
compulsive
impulsive
provision
transplant
disreputable

Thursday
disturbance
inheritance
reappearance
counterbalance
understatement

Friday
disobedient
disagreement
refurbishment
discontent
intermittent

Week 28

Monday
omelette
mauve
trouper
limousine
chauffeur

Tuesday
solitaire
cassette
rectangle
reflex
tendon

Wednesday
fuchsia
opaque
khaki
aquarium
courier

Thursday
unreasonable
remarkable
agreeable
detestable
breakable

Friday
amazement
spectate
irritated
enable
gable

sympathy • variation
responsible • disreputable
intermittent

limousine • chauffeur
aquarium • fuchsia
courier

Week 29

Monday

eloquent
eloquence
agency
adolescent
adolescence

Tuesday

precedent
precedence
tendency
salient
salience

Wednesday

negligent
negligence
malevolent
malevolence
currency

Thursday

non-violent
violence
transparency
constituency
allowance

Friday

re-enactment
believable
biodegradable
non-biodegradable
eco-friendly

Week 30

nuisance
grievance
interfere
interference
preferable

confer
conference
transference
transferable
inferior

thoroughly
trough
slough
wrought
breakthrough

knowledgeable
acknowledge
acknowledgement
undoubtable
redoubtable

hymn
column
slaughter
haughty
taught

Spell it again . . .

adolescence • salient
constituency • believable
non-biodegradable

preferable • thoroughly
breakthrough • acknowledgement
haughty

Week 31

income
perimeter
insight
decrepit
impatience

disgusting
geography
protagonist
interrupted
improvement

incredulity
universe
distribute
antagonist
overwhelmed

postpone
disappointment
embedded
discourage
selfless

decrease
overweight
extraordinary
disown
disintegrated

Week 32

painless
plentiful
rudeness
politely
cleanliness

sleepiness
ownership
speechless
powerless
flawless

lineage
portable
dreadful
successful
pearlescent

durable
pitiful
skilful
skilfully
sizeable

laudable
heaviness
saleable
weariness
downloadable

impatience • incredulity
overwhelmed • disappointment
extraordinary

cleanliness • lineage
pearlescent • sizeable
laudable

	Week 33	Week 34
Monday	ostentatious gracious precious semi-precious licentious	enhance finance financial substantial facial
Tuesday	loquacious audacious vivacious luscious spacious	glacial commercial beneficial sacrificial superficial
Wednesday	suspicious unsuspicious ferocious atrocious unconscionable	sociable unsociable unsocial antisocial racial
Thursday	unconscious self-conscious subconscious semi-conscious flirtatious	magnificent magnificence significant insignificant significance
Friday	capacious rapacious precocious tenacious pernicious	despondent despondence despondency buoyant buoyancy

Spell it again . . .

ostentatious • loquacious
unsuspicious • unconscionable
pernicious

commercial • unsociable
magnificent • despondent
buoyancy

Week 35

non-refundable
pre-eminent
predominant
predominance
predicament

countryside
alleyway
wholemeal
matchstick
swordfish

forthright
earrings
saucepan
earache
tablespoon

blackcurrant
redcurrant
freelance
newsagents
grandparent

sixpence
timetable
turntable
afterthought
forethought

Week 36

intelligent
unintelligent
intelligence
unintelligible
intelligible

dependent
dependence
independent
undependable
ambulances

convenient
convenience
inconvenient
inconvenience
resemblance

repugnant
repugnance
obedient
disobedience
obedience

succulent
succulence
confidant
self-confidence
overconfidence

Monday
Tuesday
Wednesday
Thursday
Friday

pre-eminent • alleyway
earrings • blackcurrant
forethought

intelligible • independent
convenient • disobedience
succulent

	Week 37	Week 38
Monday	resilient resilience abundant abundance pungency	abhorrent abhorrence iridescent iridescence brilliance
Tuesday	correspondent correspondence corresponding poignant poignancy	luminescent luminance luminescence extravagant extravagance
Wednesday	reminiscent reminiscence repent repentant repentance	turbulent turbulence luxuriant luxurious luxuriance
Thursday	resonant resonance proficient proficiency covalence	insistent insistence consistent consistency relevance
Friday	insurgent insurgence ambivalent ambivalence surveillance	exuberant exuberance repellent persistent persistence

Spell it again . . .

resilient • poignancy
reminiscence • covalence
surveillance

abhorrent • iridescence
luxuriant • consistent
exuberance

Week 39

Monday

voracious
capricious
fallacious
avaricious
perspicacious

Tuesday

judicious
veracious
specious
overcautious
incautious

Wednesday

auspicious
inauspicious
pugnacious
scrumptious
superstitious

Thursday

surreptitious
rumbunctious
vexatious
conscientious
facetious

Friday

contentious
fractious
pretence
pretentious
unpretentious

Week 40

pyjamas
cynical
sycamore
physician
mysterious

amethyst
acrylic
rhythmic
syllable
monosyllable

sovereign
villains
metaphor
trapezium
laboratory

microscopic
croissant
sextant
cognizance
phosphorescent

incandescent
belligerent
omnipresent
manoeuvrable
juggernaut

perspicacious • inauspicious
conscientious • surreptitious
unpretentious

amethyst • sovereign
laboratory • manoeuvrable
incandescent

Now practise . . .

Making adjectives with -able

presentable

pliable

approachable

miserable

distinguishable

exceptionable

comfortable

biodegradable

liable

downloadable

remarkable

believable

agreeable

irremediable

redoubtable

interminable

notable

imaginable

reliable

formidable

discreditable

pardonable

honourable

transferable

sociable

breakable

detestable

durable

preferable

knowledgeable

Now practise . . .

Making nouns with -ment

encouragement employment

enlightenment deployment fulfilment

containment department establishment

pronouncement banishment catchment

disagreement amazement predicament

acknowledgement

management advertisement

appointment enjoyment entertainment

accomplishment refreshment shipment

development settlement refurbishment

re-enactment embarrassment understatement

disappointment

Spelling help

Adding a prefix to make antonyms

A **prefix** is a group of letters that is added to the **beginning** of a root word to make a new word.

Adding the prefixes **-un** or **-dis** can change a word to give it the opposite meaning. Words with opposite meanings are called **antonyms.**

Here are some words with the prefixes **-un** or **-dis** that you have already learned to spell in this book.

obedience / **dis**obedience	acceptable / **un**acceptable
appearance / **dis**appearance	suitable / **un**suitable
treatable / **un**treatable	employment /**un**employment
salvageable / **un**salvageable	fortunately / **un**fortunately
manageable / **un**manageable	questionable / **un**questionable

Have a look at page **60** of **Better Spelling 1** for other words with prefixes.

-ise or -ize?

Which is right? Is it **-ize** or **-ise**?
Most words ending in **-ise** or **-ize** can be spelled either way in English in the UK. You might see any of these words spelled with an **-ize** or **-ise** ending.

apologise / apologize	hypnotise / hypnotize
civilise / civilize	specialise / specialize
monopolise / monopolize	sympathise / sympathize

However some words can only be spelled with an **-ise** ending. These words are:

advertise	disguise	improvise

Spelling help

Tricky spellings

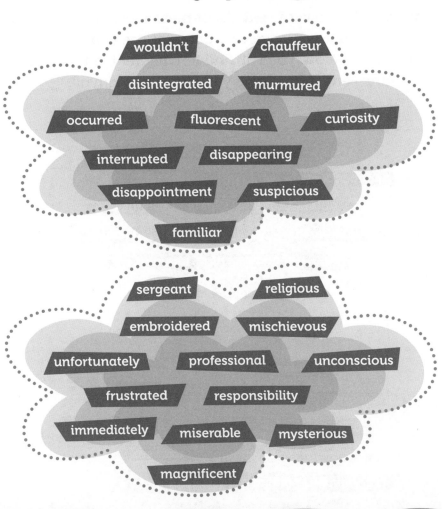

wouldn't

chauffeur

disintegrated

murmured

occurred

fluorescent

curiosity

interrupted

disappearing

disappointment

suspicious

familiar

sergeant

religious

embroidered

mischievous

unfortunately

professional

unconscious

frustrated

responsibility

immediately

miserable

mysterious

magnificent

Based on the Oxford Children's Corpus research
and analysis. See pp94-95 for more information.

Word fun

Making rhymes with -ent

Many words end with **-ent**. All of these words rhyme with each other but can have very different spelling patterns. In the words below, you will find ten different letters before the **-ent** suffix. See if you can spot them all.

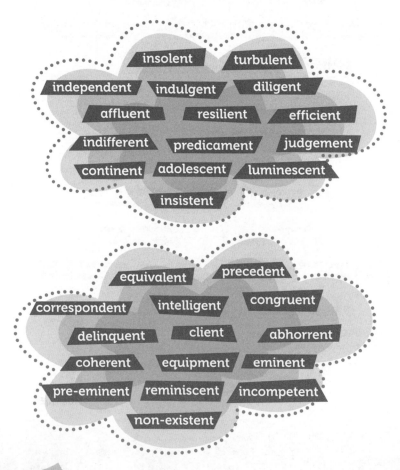

insolent
turbulent
independent
indulgent
diligent
affluent
resilient
efficient
indifferent
predicament
judgement
continent
adolescent
luminescent
insistent

equivalent
precedent
correspondent
intelligent
congruent
delinquent
client
abhorrent
coherent
equipment
eminent
pre-eminent
reminiscent
incompetent
non-existent

Word fun

Words within a word

Sometimes you can find small words inside big words. Each of the words below has at least five small words in it. Match each word to each group of five words in the clouds below.

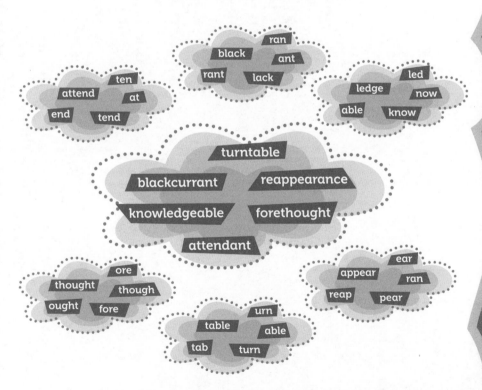